RUBANK EDUCATIONAL LIBRARY No. 179

Advanced Method

TROMBONE OR BARITONE

VOL. II

WM. GOWER
AND
H. VOXMAN

AN OUTLINED COURSE OF STUDY
DESIGNED TO FOLLOW UP ANY
OF THE VARIOUS ELEMENTARY
AND INTERMEDIATE METHODS

RUBANK®

HAL•LEONARD®
CORPORATION

NOTE

THE RUBANK ADVANCED METHOD for Trombone or Baritone is published in two volumes, the course of study being divided in the following manner:

Vol. I { Keys of Bb, Eb, F, Ab, and C Major.
{ Keys of G, C, D, F, and A Minor.

Vol. II { Keys of Db, G, Gb, D, Cb, and A Major.
{ Keys of Bb, E, Eb, and B Minor.

PREFACE

THIS METHOD is designed to follow any of the various Elementary and Intermediate instruction series, or Elementary instruction series comprising two or more volumes, depending upon the previous development of the student. The authors have found it necessary in their teaching experience to draw from many sources in order to provide a progressive course of study. The present publication assembles in two volumes, the material essential to a well-rounded musical development.

THE OUTLINES, one of which is included in each of the respective volumes, tend to afford an objective picture of the student's progress. They will facilitate the ranking of members in a large ensemble or they may serve as a basis for awards of merit. In addition, a one-sided development along strictly technical or strictly melodic lines is avoided. The use of these outlines, however, is not imperative and they may be discarded at the discretion of the teacher.

Wm. Gower — H. Voxman

Chromatic Chart for Trombone and Baritone

① The B♮ or C♭ in the staff is too sharp. Flatten this tone enough to make it in good tune.

② The C above the staff will be too flat. Shorten the position on the trombone enough to make it in tune.
   On the baritone the first and third valves may be used in slow passages to correct this pitch.

③ The D above the staff is sometimes too flat. Use first and second valves on baritone or fourth position on trombone to correct this.

④ The G above the staff in the second position on trombone must be made in short second (2-) to be in tune.

⑤ The F# or G♭ above the staff in the third position on trombone must be made in short third (3-).

TABLE OF HARMONICS

The Bass Trombone

THE F ATTACHMENT

The modern bass trombone is basically a Bb instrument like the tenor trombone. It differs from the tenor trombone in having a larger bore, a bell of wider diameter, and an attachment of two extra turns of tubing which is in itself equivalent in length to the tube length of the sixth position. The extra tubing is connected with the basic tubing by means of a valve that is operated with the thumb of the left hand. The purpose of this mechanism is to increase the downward range of the instrument, or to replace the sixth position in order to avoid long rapid shifts of the slide.

This attachment is called the F attachment, since low F may be played in the first position with the thumb valve closed (depressed). The slide positions on the trombone are employed sequentially to descend chromatically, but when the F attachment is used the positions become spaced further apart, with the result that only six positions are usable instead of seven. The distances between the positions become approximately 4¾ inches as compared to the normal 3⅛ inches. Thus, the total length of the slide is reached in the sixth position.

The main point in favor of this system with the F attachment is that the player is enabled to use the thumb valve in preference to the sixth position, and the thumb valve with second position in place of the seventh position, when long shifts are involved. With this system, low B natural (𝄢) is not playable, although it is sometimes called for in orchestral parts for the bass trombone. Because of this limitation the use of the E attachment is recommended.

THE E ATTACHMENT

Most modern bass trombones have a tuning slide in the F attachment sufficiently long so that it may be tuned down to E natural (𝄢). After this is done, all tones formerly played in the seventh position of the Bb trombone are playable in the first position with the thumb valve closed (depressed). Thus, low E natural (𝄢) is played in the first position with the thumb valve, the second position is dropped entirely, and Eb is played in the third position with the valve. This system, except for the first position, numbers the positions for the tones the same as they are numbered an octave higher:

The positions for these lower tones, however, must not be considered identical in placement with those an octave higher. The player must use his ear to guide him in spacing them correctly.

The tones made possible by the use of the attachments are those between the limits of the first and second harmonics.

T = thumb valve. The numerals indicate the positions.

Below the range indicated above, the pedal tones (fundamental tones) may be employed to descend to the lowest E natural, the fundamental of the seventh position. The positions for the pedal tones are identical to those for the tones an octave higher. The thumb valve is not used.

A somewhat different control of the embouchure is necessary in each of the registers, but the player must endeavor to keep the same quality of tone in passing from one register to another at all times.

OUTLINE
OF
RUBANK ADVANCED METHOD
FOR
TROMBONE, Vol. II
BY
Wm. Gower and H. Voxman

UNIT	SCALES and ARPEGGIOS		(Key)	MELODIC INTERPRETATION	ARTICULATION	FLEXIBILITY and TONGUING		ORNAMENTS — CLEF STUDIES	SOLOS	UNIT COMPLETED
1	9 (1) 10 (5)		Db	24 (1)	53 (1)	68 (1)	72 (1)	77 (1)	87 (1)	
2	9 (2) 10 (6)		Db	25 (2)	53 (2)	68 (1)	72 (1)	77 (2)	87 (1)	
3	9 (3) 10 (7)		Db	26 (3)	54 (3)	68 (1)	72 (2)	77 (2)	87 (1)	
4	10 (4) (8)		Db	26 (4)	54 (3)	68 (2)	72 (3)	77 (3)	87 (1)	
5	10 (9) 11 (12)		bb	28 (5)	55 (4)	68 (2)	72 (4)	77 (3)	87 (1)	
6	11 (10) (13)		bb	29 (6)	55 (5)	68 (2)	72 (4)	77 (4)	87 (1)	
7	11 (11) (14)		bb	30 (7)	56 (6)	69 (3)	72 (5)	78 (5)	88 (2)	
8	12 (15) 13 (18)		G	30 (8)	56 (7)	69 (3)	72 (5)	78 (5)	88 (2)	
9	12 (16) 13 (19)		G	31 (9)	57 (8)	69 (4)	73 (6)	78 (6)	88 (2)	
10	12 (17)		G	31 (10)	57 (9)	69 (4)	73 (6)	78 (7)	88 (2)	
11	13 (20) (21)		G	32 (11)	58 (10)	69 (5)	73 (7)	78 (7)	88 (2)	
12	13 (22) 14 (25)		e	33 (12A)	58 (11)	69 (5)	73 (7)	79 (8) (9)	88 (2)	
13	13 (23) 14 (26)		e	35 (13)	58 (12)	69 (6)	73 (8)	79 (10)	90 (3A)	
14	14 (24) (27) (28)		e	35 (13)	59 (13)	69 (6)	73 (8)	79 (11)	90 (3A)	
15	15 (29)		Gb	36 (14)	59 (14)	69 (6)	74 (9)	79 (11)	90 (3A)	
16	15 (30) 16 (33)		Gb	37 (15)	59 (15)	69 (6)	74 (9)	80 (12) (13)	90 (3A)	
17	15 (31) 16 (34)		Gb	38 (16)	60 (16)	69 (7)	74 (9)	80 (14)	90 (3A)	
18	16 (32) (35)		Gb	39 (17)	60 (17)	69 (7)	74 (10)	80 (15)	90 (3A)	
19	16 (36) 17 (37)		eb	40 (18)	60 (18)	69 (7)	74 (10)	80 (16)	92 (4)	
20	17 (38) (40)		eb	40 (19)	61 (19)	70 (8)	74 (11)	80 (16)	92 (4)	
21	17 (39) (41) (42)		eb	41 (20)	61 (19)	70 (8)	74 (11)	80 (17)	92 (4)	
22	18 (43) 19 (46)		D	42 (21)	62 (20A)	70 (8)	75 (12)	80 (17)	92 (4)	
23	18 (44)		D	42 (22)	62 (21)	70 (8)	75 (12)	81 (18A)	92 (4)	
24	18 (45)		D	44 (23)	63 (22A)	70 (8)	75 (13)	81 (18A)	92 (4)	
25	19 (47) (48)		D	44 (23)	63 (22A)	70 (9)	75 (14)	82 (19)	94 (5)	
26	19 (49) (50)		b	45 (24)	64 (23)	70 (9)	75 (14)	82 (20) (21)	94 (5)	
27	19 (51) 20 (53) (54)		b	45 (24)	64 (24)	70 (9)	75 (15)	82 (21)	94 (5)	
28	20 (52) (55)		b	47 (25)	64 (25)	70 (9)	75 (15)	84 (31)	94 (5)	
29	20 (56) 22 (60)		Cb	49 (26A)	65 (26)	70 (9)	76 (16)	84 (32)	94 (5)	
30	21 (57) 22 (61)		Cb	49 (26A)	65 (27)	70 (9)	76 (16)	85 (1) (2)	94 (5)	
31	21 (58) 22 (62)		Cb	50 (27)	66 (28)	71 (10)	76 (17)	85 (3)	95 (6)	
32	21 (59) 22 (63)		Cb	50 (27)	66 (28)	71 (10)	76 (17)	85 (4)	95 (6)	
33	22 (64)		A	50 (28)	66 (29)	71 (10)	76 (18)	86 (5)	95 (6)	
34	23 (65) (68)		A	51 (29)	67 (30)	71 (10)	76 (18)	86 (6)	95 (6)	
35	23 (66) (69)		A	52 (30)	67 (31)	71 (10)	76 (19)	86 (7)	95 (6)	
36	23 (67) (70)		A	52 (30)	67 (32)	71 (10)	76 (19)	86 (7)	95 (6)	

NUMERALS designate page number.

ENCIRCLED NUMERALS designate exercise number.

COMPLETED EXERCISES may be indicated by crossing out the rings, thus,

OUTLINE
OF
RUBANK ADVANCED METHOD
FOR
BARITONE, Vol. II
BY
Wm. Gower and H. Voxman

UNIT	SCALES and ARPEGGIOS (Key)	MELODIC INTERPRE-TATION	ARTICU-LATION	FLEXIBILITY and TONGUING	ORNA-MENTS	SOLOS	UNIT COM-PLETED
1	9 (1) 10 (5) Db	24 (1)	53 (1)	68 (1) 72 (1)	77 (1)	87 (1)	
2	9 (2) 10 (6) Db	25 (2)	53 (2)	68 (1) 72 (1)	77 (2)	87 (1)	
3	9 (3) 10 (7) Db	26 (3)	54 (3)	68 (1) 72 (2)	77 (2)	87 (1)	
4	10 (4) (8) Db	26 (4)	54 (3)	68 (2) 72 (3)	77 (3)	87 (1)	
5	10 (9) 11 (12) bb	28 (5)	55 (4)	68 (2) 72 (4)	77 (3)	87 (1)	
6	11 (10) (13) bb	29 (6)	55 (5)	68 (2) 72 (4)	77 (4)	87 (1)	
7	11 (11) (14) bb	30 (7)	56 (6)	69 (3) 72 (5)	78 (5)	88 (2)	
8	12 (15) 13 (18) G	30 (8)	56 (7)	69 (3) 72 (5)	78 (5)	88 (2)	
9	12 (16) 13 (19) G	31 (9)	57 (8)	69 (4) 73 (6)	78 (6)	88 (2)	
10	12 (17) G	31 (10)	57 (9)	69 (4) 73 (6)	78 (7)	88 (2)	
11	13 (20) (21) G	32 (11)	58 (10)	69 (5) 73 (7)	78 (7)	88 (2)	
12	13 (22) 14 (25) e	33 (12)	58 (11)	69 (5) 73 (7)	79 (8) (9)	88 (2)	
13	13 (23) 14 (26) e	35 (13)	58 (12)	69 (6) 73 (8)	79 (10)	89 (3)	
14	14 (24) (27) (28) e	35 (13)	59 (13)	69 (6) 73 (8)	79 (11)	89 (3)	
15	15 (29) Gb	36 (14)	59 (14)	69 (6) 74 (9)	79 (11)	89 (3)	
16	15 (30) 16 (33) Gb	37 (15)	59 (15)	69 (6) 74 (9)	80 (12) (13)	89 (3)	
17	15 (31) 16 (34) Gb	38 (16)	60 (16)	69 (7) 74 (9)	80 (14)	89 (3)	
18	16 (32) (35) Gb	39 (17)	60 (17)	69 (7) 74 (10)	80 (15)	89 (3)	
19	16 (36) 17 (37) eb	40 (18)	60 (18)	69 (7) 74 (10)	80 (16)	92 (4)	
20	17 (38) (40) eb	40 (19)	61 (19)	70 (8) 74 (11)	80 (17)	92 (4)	
21	17 (39) (41) (42) eb	41 (20)	61 (19)	70 (8) 74 (11)	80 (17)	92 (4)	
22	18 (43) 19 (46) D	42 (21)	61 (20)	70 (8) 75 (12)	81 (18)	92 (4)	
23	18 (44) D	42 (22)	62 (21)	70 (8) 75 (12)	81 (18)	92 (4)	
24	18 (45) D	44 (23)	62 (22)	70 (8) 75 (13)	82 (19)	92 (4)	
25	19 (47) (48) D	44 (23)	62 (22)	70 (9) 75 (14)	82 (20)	94 (5)	
26	19 (49) (50) b	45 (24)	64 (23)	70 (9) 75 (14)	82 (21)	94 (5)	
27	19 (51) 20 (53) (54) b	45 (24)	64 (24)	70 (9) 75 (15)	82 (21)	94 (5)	
28	20 (52) (55) b	47 (25)	64 (25)	70 (9) 75 (15)	83 (22)	94 (5)	
29	20 (56) 22 (60) Cb	48 (26)	65 (26)	70 (9) 76 (16)	83 (23)	94 (5)	
30	21 (57) 22 (61) Cb	48 (26)	65 (27)	70 (9) 76 (16)	83 (24)	94 (5)	
31	21 (58) 22 (62) Cb	50 (27)	66 (28)	71 (10) 76 (17)	83 (24)	95 (6)	
32	21 (59) 22 (63) Cb	50 (27)	66 (28)	71 (10) 76 (17)	84 (25) (26)	95 (6)	
33	22 (64) A	50 (28)	66 (29)	71 (10) 76 (18)	84 (27) (28)	95 (6)	
34	23 (65) (68) A	51 (29)	67 (30)	71 (10) 76 (18)	84 (29) (30)	95 (6)	
35	23 (66) (69) A	52 (30)	67 (31)	71 (10) 76 (19)	84 (31)	95 (6)	
36	23 (67) (70) A	52 (30)	67 (32)	71 (10) 76 (19)	84 (32)	95 (6)	

NUMERALS designate page number.
ENCIRCLED NUMERALS designate exercise number.
COMPLETED EXERCISES may be indicated by crossing out the rings, thus,

PRACTICE AND GRADE REPORT

SECOND SEMESTER

Student's Name _____

Date _____

Week	Sun.	Mon.	Tue.	Wed.	Thu.	Fri.	Sat.	Total	Parent's Signature	Grade
1										
2										
3										
4										
5										
6										
7										
8										
9										
10										
11										
12										
13										
14										
15										
16										
17										
18										
19										
20										

Semester Grade _____

Instructor's Signature _____

FIRST SEMESTER

Student's Name _____

Date _____

Week	Sun.	Mon.	Tue.	Wed.	Thu.	Fri.	Sat.	Total	Parent's Signature	Grade
1										
2										
3										
4										
5										
6										
7										
8										
9										
10										
11										
12										
13										
14										
15										
16										
17										
18										
19										
20										

Semester Grade _____

Instructor's Signature _____

Scales and Arpeggios

Db Major

* 4- indicates short 4th position; numbers above notes are for trombone only.

10

Use different articulations

Various articulations may be used in the chromatic, the interval, and the arpeggio exercises.

Chromatic Scale

Exercise in Thirds

Common Chord

Dominant 7th Chord

B♭ Minor

Natural   Harmonic

Melodic

Exercise in Thirds

Common Chord

Diminished 7th Chord

G Major

Chromatic Scale

Exercise in Thirds

Common Chord

Diminished 7th Chord

Gb Major

D Major

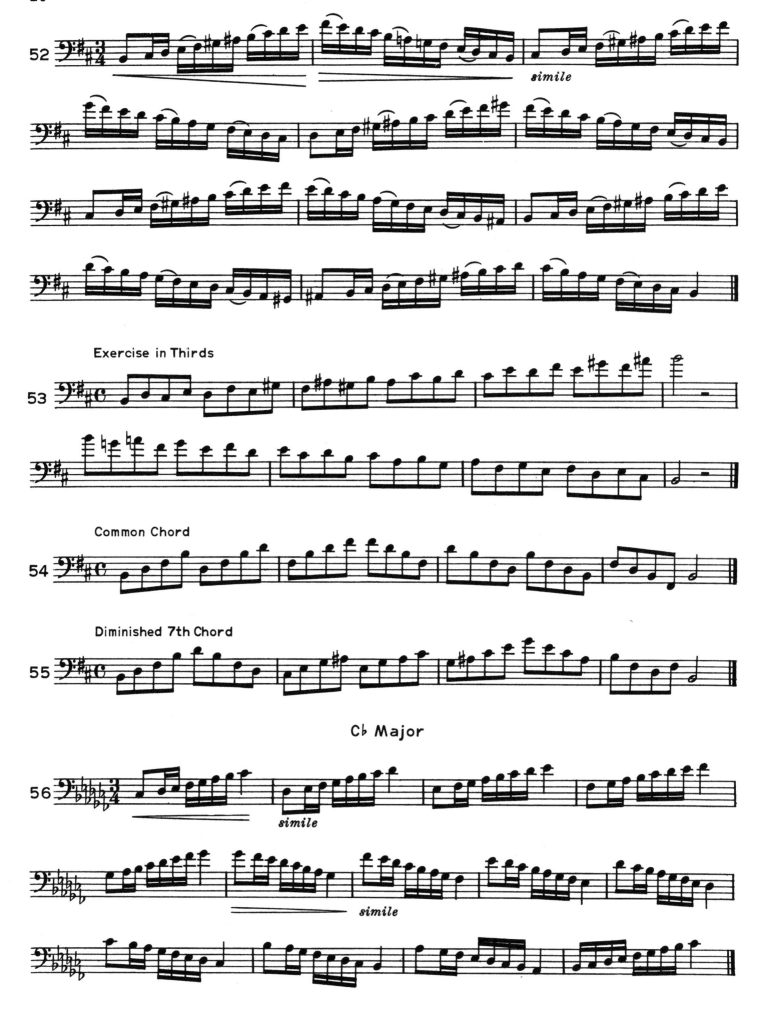

Exercise in Thirds

Common Chord

Diminished 7th Chord

Cb Major

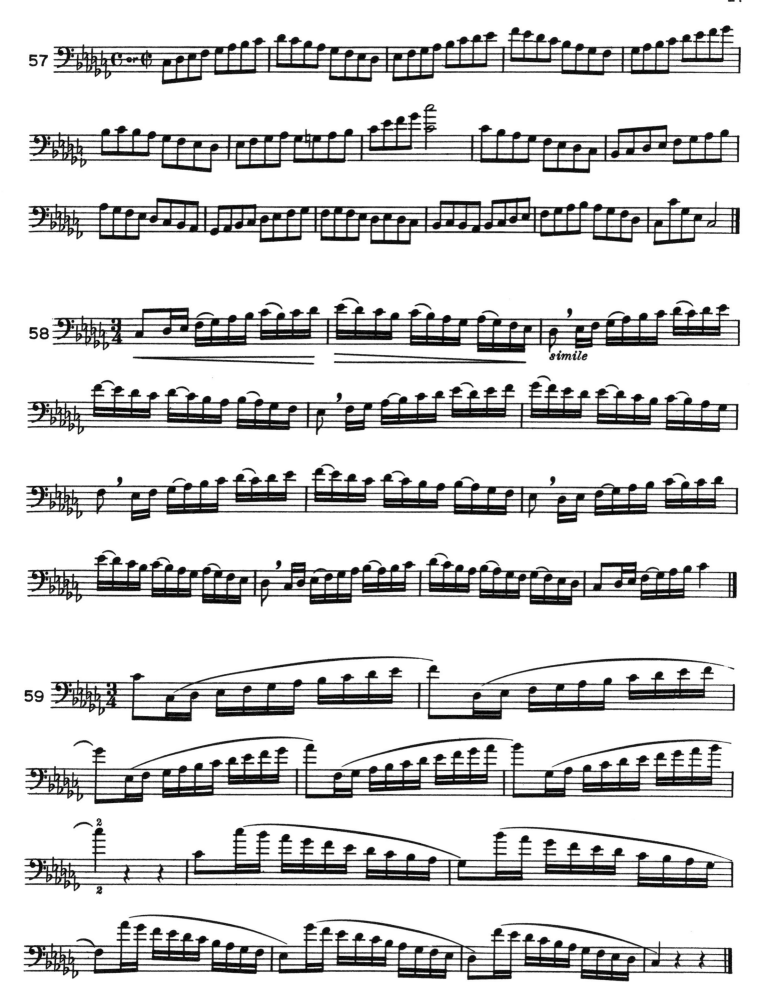

Exercise in Thirds
Practice also octave lower

Common Chord

Dominant 7th Chord

Studies in Melodic Interpretation
For One or Two Part Playing

The following studies have been selected with the idea of ensemble performance in mind. Much effort has been expended in selecting duets in which the first and second parts are melodically and rhythmically independent. Students should be encouraged to practice these numbers as duets outside of the lesson period. When circumstances permit, any number of students can perform them as an ensemble. The lower part of the duets may be assigned at the discretion of the teacher.

Careful attention to the marks of expression is essential to effective use of the material. Where different dynamic signs are written for the upper and lower parts, observe them accurately. The part having the melody must always slightly predominate even when the dynamic indications are the same.

Pencil the technically difficult passages and devote extra time to their mastery.

In rhythmic music in the more rapid tempi (marches, dances, etc.) tones that are equal divisions of the beat are played somewhat detached (staccato). Tones that equal a beat or are multiples of a beat are held full value. Tones followed by rests are usually held full value. This point should be especially observed in slow music.

Trills and other ornaments may be omitted by the trombonist at the discretion of the teacher.

TESSARINI

Allegretto

RAMAIN

2

* Numbers above notes are for trombone only (positions).

Aria

(from King Arthur)

PURCELL

GATTI

Air

18th Century

Andante (in three)

GOSTINELLI

Air
(Lovely Nancy)

Old English

Jigg

Old English

FESTING

Allegro vivace

Allemande

The + is the symbol for a trill.

BOISMORTIER

HENNING

* Baritone only.
** Trombone only.

Gavot

18th Century

[Allegretto]

14

BRUNI

Allegretto

Bourrée

18th Century

PLEYEL - BLUME

Andante

17

Andantino

SCHUMANN

GOSTINELLI

Courante

BOISMORTIER

Giga

18th Century

Scherzo

HENNING

Marziale

Andante sostenuto

HENNING

24

48

Allegro [in four]

* 26

* Baritone only.

HASSE

Lively

** Trombone only.

BOISMORTIER

Andante [in eight]

27

Bridal Song

Russian

Sostenuto

28

Allegretto

30

Poco meno

Studies in Articulation

The material for this section has been taken from standard methods for trombone, baritone, and other brass instruments.

In all exercises where no tempo is indicated the student should play the study as rapidly as is consistent with tonal control and technical accuracy. The first practice on each exercise should be done very slowly in order that the articulation may be carefully observed.

In allegro tempi figures similar to 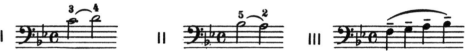 should be performed , etc.

The figure should be played .

The slur is a difficult articulation on the slide trombone. Whenever possible, the motion of the slide should be outward when playing an ascending slurred passage (Ex. I), and inward when playing a descending slurred passage (Ex. II).

When it is not possible to move the slide as recommended above, the tones under the slur should be tongued as lightly as possible, fully sustained, and free of any trace of glissando. See Ex. III.

Play the exercises as quickly as technic permits unless otherwise indicated.

Allegro moderato

* Numbers above notes are for trombones only (positions).

57

Tempo di marcia

Practice with different articulations.

* Baritone only.

62

Allegro assai

**22
A

[rit]

p a tempo

dim.

cresc.

** Trombones only.

Also practice No. 26: (1) ♩♪♪♪ (2) ♪♪♪♩ (3) ♪♪♪♪

Also practice No. 30: (1) (2) (3)

Flexibility Exercises

Trombone positions are noted above the staff, baritone fingerings below.

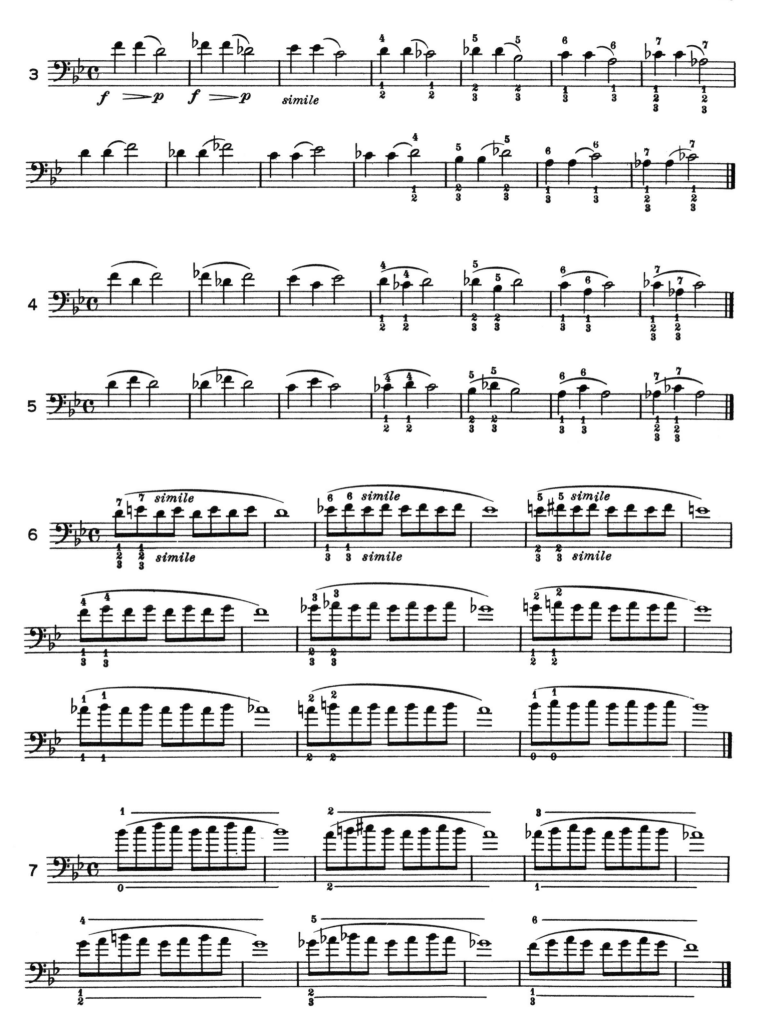

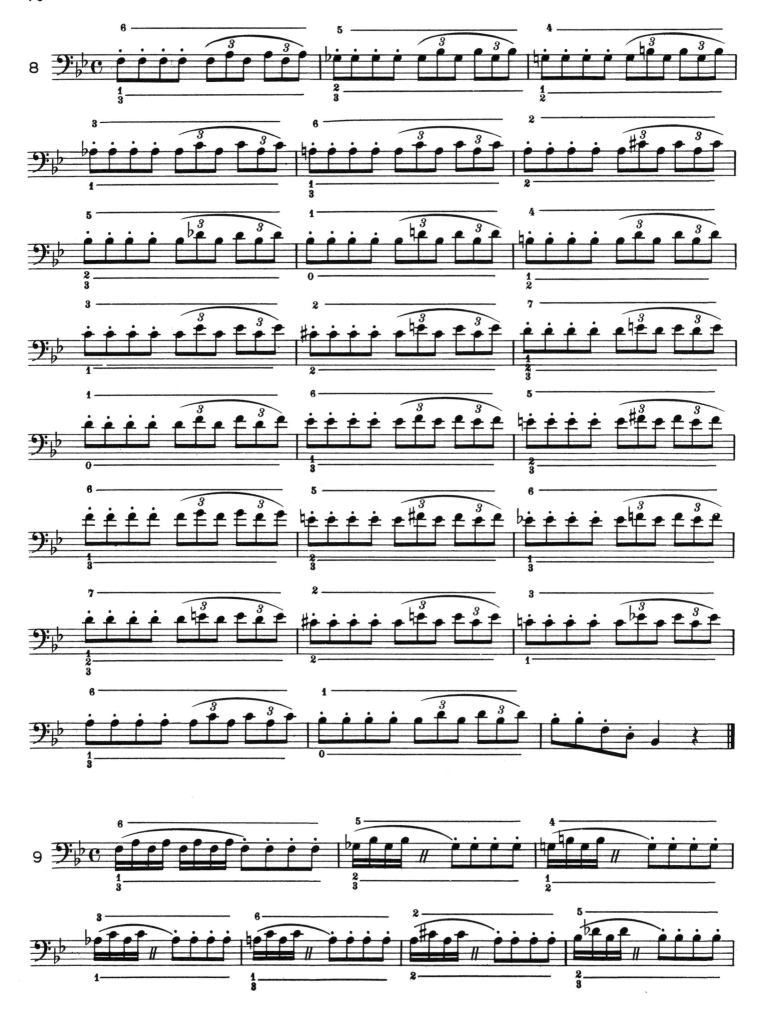

Tonguing Exercises
TRIPLE TONGUING and DOUBLE TONGUING

Triple tonguing is used when triplets are to be played at a speed that is too fast for single tonguing. The pattern of syllables used for this kind of tonguing is: Tu Tu Ku, Tu Tu Ku, etc.

Double tonguing is used when duplets are to be played at a speed that is too fast for single tonguing. The pattern of syllables in this case is: Tu Ku, Tu Ku, etc.

To develop a technique for either Triple or Double Tonguing it is **recommended** that the Ku attacks be practiced separately from the Tu attacks until a good tone can be produced on both syllables. The student may then proceed to combine the Tu and Ku, being particularly careful that both syllables sound equally distinct. It is advisable to practice slowly at first in order to produce an evenly articulated rhythm. Increase to a faster tempo only as perfection is reached.

PREPARATORY STUDIES

TRIPLE TONGUING

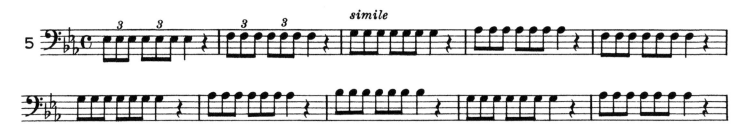

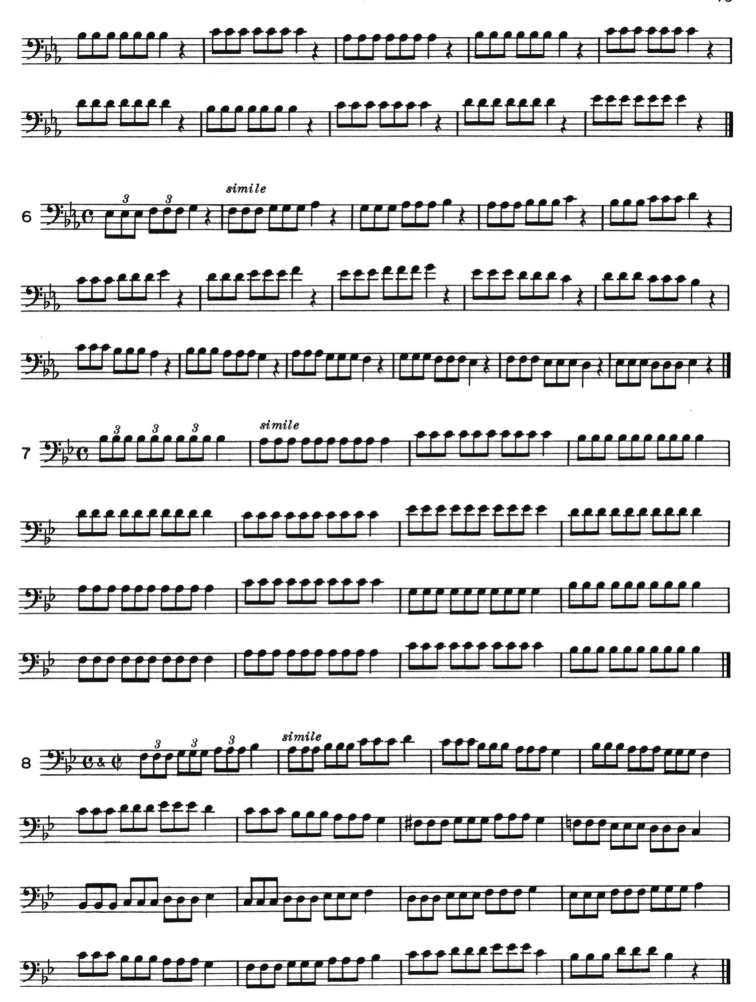

DOUBLE TONGUING

Musical Ornamentation (Embellishments)

The execution of many ornaments is not feasible on the slide trombone, for example, most trills. From the standpoint of the trombonist's musical development, however, he must acquaint himself with the interpretation of the commonly used embellishments. Refer to the trombone outline for exercises to be used.

78

Allegretto

5

Allegretto

6

Allegretto

Be sure to play the mordent squarely on the beat:

7

Long Grace Notes (Appoggiatura)

The Turn (Gruppetto)

GALLAY

Two Excerpts from "Lohengrin"

WAGNER

KLOSÉ

* Baritone only.
** Trombone only.

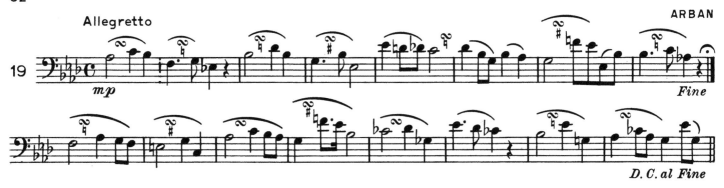

In the music of Wagner it is sometimes necessary to play turns that begin on the lower instead of the upper note. The symbol for this inverted turn is ∾. The turn in the excerpt from "Rienzi" was not written thus originally by Wagner but is usually interpreted in the manner indicated.

In the music of the time of Bach and Handel (1685-1759), cadences frequently contain the rhythmic figure ⟨fig⟩ or ⟨fig⟩. The time value of the dot is not trilled, the execution being ⟨fig⟩ etc. It should be added that the trills of this period should generally begin with the upper note of the trill.

Saraband

* Baritone only.

* Baritone only.

Tenor Clef Studies

The tenor clef  is a C clef so used as to indicate middle C on the fourth line of the staff.

Allegro

5

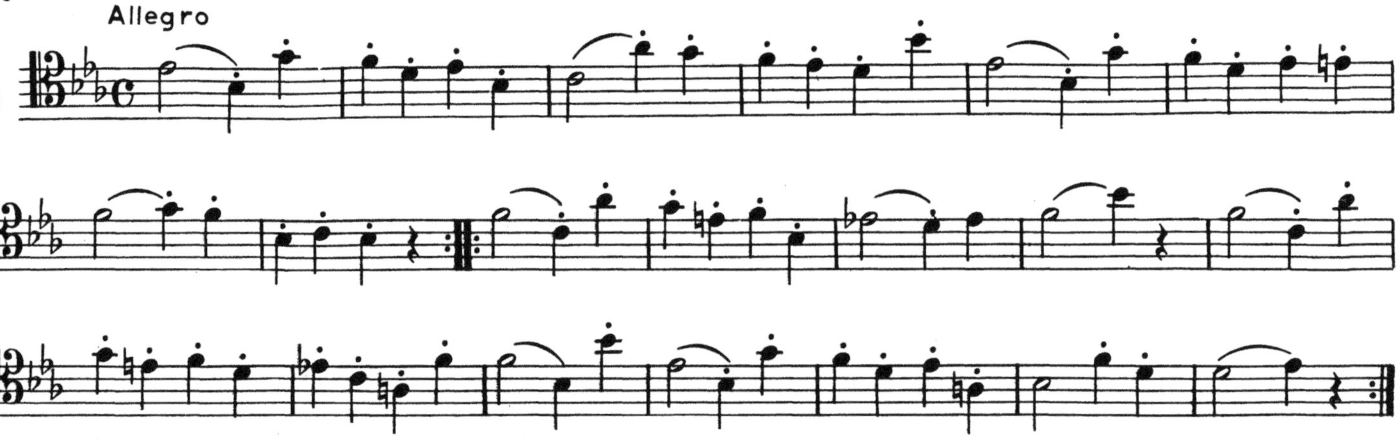

Allegretto

6

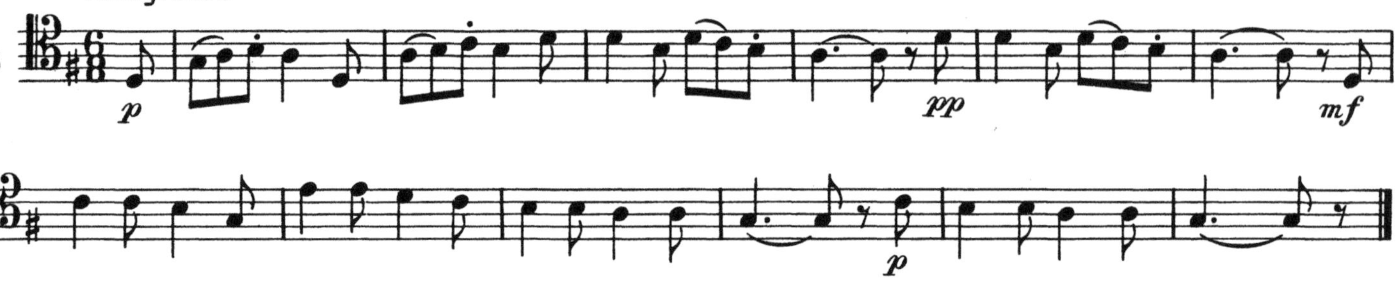

Moderato

7

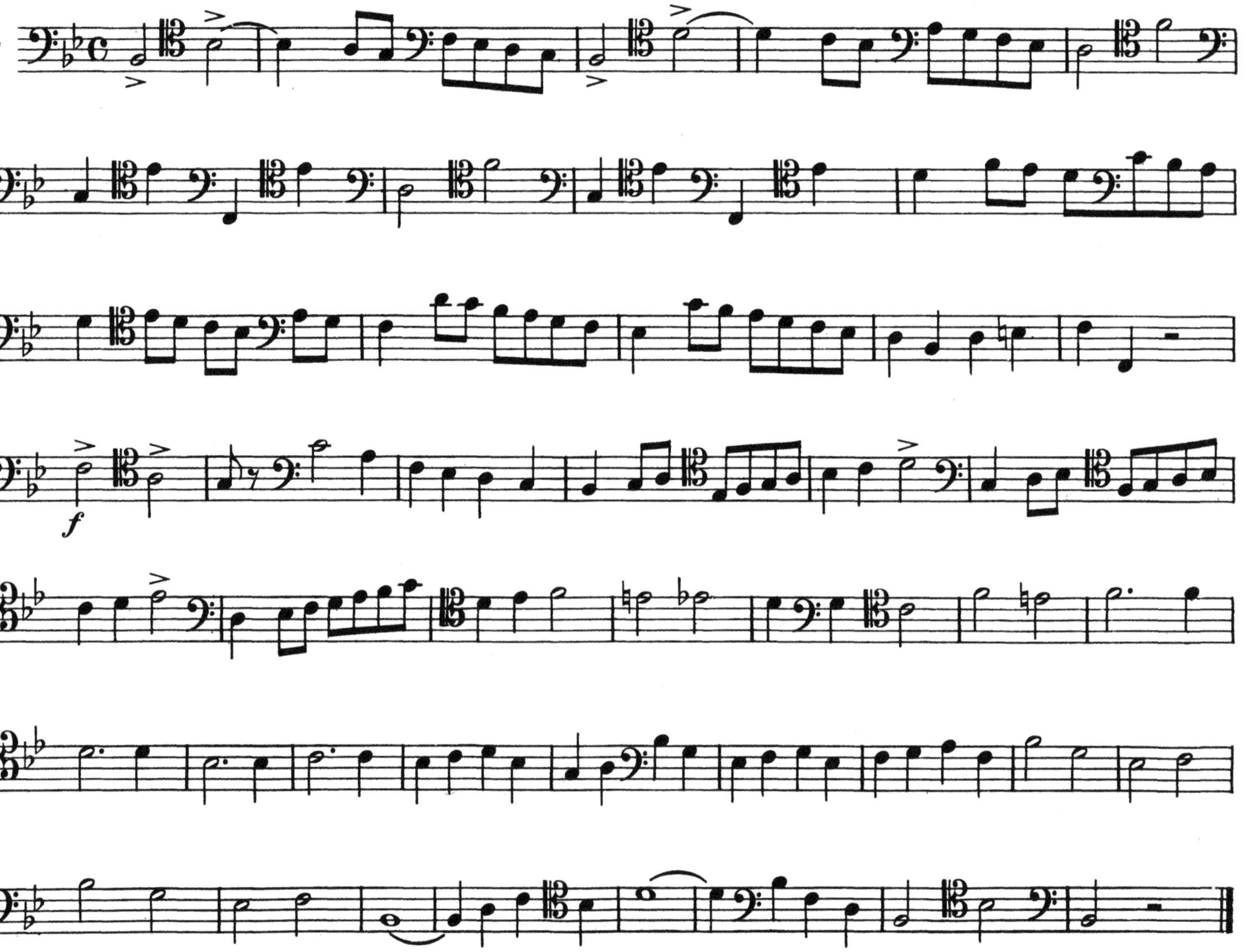

SOLOS
Salve Maria

Solo Trombone or Baritone

S. MERCADANTE

Romanze

Solo Trombone or Baritone

EDMUND GUMPERT, Op.19

Petite Pièce Concertante

Solo Baritone

G. BALAY

Love Thoughts

Solo Trombone

ARTHUR PRYOR
Transcribed by Clair W. Johnson

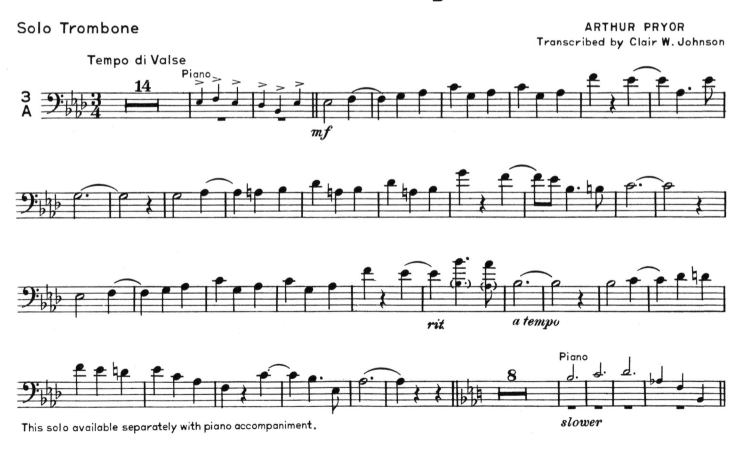

This solo available separately with piano accompaniment.

Morceau de Concours

Solo Trombone or Baritone

G. ALARY, Op. 57

Crépuscule
(Twilight)

Solo Trombone or Baritone

GABRIEL PARÈS

Concerto in F Minor

Solo Trombone or Baritone

E. LAUGA

NOTE: Piano accompaniments to Nos. 2, 3A, 4, 5, and 6 are included in the Piano book to the "Concert and Contest Collection for Trombone." Likewise, the Piano accompaniments to Nos. 3 and 4 are included in the Piano book to the "Concert and Contest Collection for B♭ Cornet, Trumpet or Baritone."